3 0400 00598 537 5

Airdrie
Marigold Library System

I0606208

Shields

Sheelagh Matthews

Weigl

Airdrie Public Library
111–304 Main Street S
Airdrie, Alberta T4B 3C3

Published by Weigl Educational Publishers Limited
6325 10th Street SE
Calgary, Alberta, Canada T2H 2Z9

Website: www.weigl.com

Copyright ©2011 Weigl Educational Publishers Limited
All rights reserved. No part of this publication may be reproduced, stored in a retrieval system, or transmitted in any form or by any means, electronic, mechanical, photocopying, recording, or otherwise, without the prior written permission of the publisher.

Library and Archives Canada Cataloguing in Publication

Matthews, Sheelagh
        Shields/ Sheelagh Matthews.
(Canadian ecozones)
Includes index.
Also available in electronic format.
ISBN 978-1-55388-628-0 (bound).--ISBN 978-1-55388-629-7 (pbk.)
        1. Natural history--Canadian Shield--Juvenile literature.
2. Ecology--Canadian Shield--Juvenile literature. 3. Occupations--
Canadian Shield--Juvenile literature. 4. Ecological zones--Canadian
Shield--Juvenile literature. 5. Canadian Shield--Juvenile literature.
I. Title. II. Series: Canadian ecozones

QH106.M38 2010   j577.09714   C2009-907292-0

Printed in the United States of America in North Mankato, Minnesota
1 2 3 4 5 6 7 8 9 0 14 13 12 11 10

072010
WEP230610

Project Coordinator
Heather Kissock

Designers
Warren Clark, Janine Vangool

Photograph Credits

Weigl acknowledges Getty Images, All Canada Photos, and Alamy as image suppliers for this title.

Every reasonable effort has been made to trace ownership and to obtain permission to reprint copyright material. The publishers would be pleased to have any errors or omissions brought to their attention so that they may be corrected in subsequent printings.

We acknowledge the financial support of the Government of Canada through the Canada Book Fund for our publishing activities.

All of the Internet URLs given in the book were valid at the time of publication. However, due to the dynamic nature of the Internet, some addresses may have changed, or sites may have ceased to exist since publication. While the author and publisher regret any inconvenience this may cause readers, no responsibility for any such changes can be accepted by either the author or the publisher.

CONTENTS

Introduction

Canada is one of the largest countries in the world and also one of the most diverse. It spans nearly 10 million square kilometres, from the Pacific Ocean in the west to the Atlantic Ocean in the east. Canada's vast landscape features a wide range of geography. Yet, as diverse as the country's geography is, some areas still share common characteristics. These regions are called ecozones. Along with common geographic features, ecozones share similar climates and life forms, such as plants and animals.

Ecozones demonstrate the reliance between **organisms** and their environment. All organisms have unique survival needs. Some organisms thrive in cold, while others require hot climates. They rely on their environment to meet their needs. Just like a puzzle, every organism has its own place in an ecozone.

The islands around Ontario's Georgian Bay feature the rocky surface of a shield ecozone.

Canada has both terrestrial, or land-based, and marine, or water-based, ecozones. The terrestrial ecozones can be grouped into five broad categories. These are Arctic, shields, plains, maritimes, and cordilleras.

Canada's shield ecozones cover much of the geographic region known as the Canadian Shield. This area extends west to Alberta, east to Labrador and north into the Northwest Territories and Nunavut.

Shields are formations of massive areas of stable, exposed, ancient **Precambrian** rock. The rocks that form the Canadian Shield were once the buried roots of tall mountains. Thick sheets of ice wore down these mountains until their roots were exposed, leaving behind relatively flat expanses of rock. These exposed roots continue to be shaped by **erosion** today. Shields occur on all continents, and they usually form the stable centre of a continental land mass.

FASCINATING FACTS

The rock found in Canada's shield ecozones is some of the oldest in the world. In the area north of Great Slave Lake, some rock is thought to be more than four billion years old.

The Canadian Shield covers about 4.8 million square kilometres of land, nearly half of Canada.

Shield Locations

Two ecozones make up most of the Canadian Shield. These are the Taiga Shield and Boreal Shield ecozones. The Taiga Shield extends into Canada's North. The Boreal Shield covers the forested areas south of the Taiga Shield.

Taiga Shield

The Taiga Shield ecozone is north of the Boreal Shield. It is separated into two parts by the Hudson Bay. The west section covers the south-central Northwest Territories, most of southern Nunavut, and northern portions of Saskatchewan and Manitoba. The eastern section covers central Quebec and most of Labrador. The northern parts of the Taiga Shield ecozone contain Canada's **tree line**, where **tundra** appears and tree growth is minimal.

Lakes and wetlands can be found in the Taiga Shield near Yellowknife, Northwest Territories.

Much of northern Ontario, including the area around Lake Superior, is part of the Boreal Shield ecozone.

Boreal Shield

The Boreal Shield ecozone covers 1.8 million square kilometres of Canada. It is the country's largest ecozone. The Boreal Shield follows a "U" shape from northern Alberta to Newfoundland. As the Boreal Shield ecozone makes its way east, it arches over Lake Winnipeg before heading south, where it runs along the northern coasts of the Great Lakes. It begins heading north again as it enters Quebec, travelling north of the St. Lawrence River through to Labrador and Newfoundland.

FASCINATING FACTS

The Boreal Shield ecozone covers about 20 percent of Canada's land mass.

The Taiga Shield covers 1.3 million square kilometres of Canada's land mass. It is the country's third-largest ecozone.

Due to its northern location, the Taiga Shield has a small population. About 35,000 people live here. Approximately 60 percent of the population is Aboriginal.

Thunder Bay, Ontario, is the largest city in the Boreal Shield ecozone. Yellowknife, the capital city of the Northwest Territories, is the largest city in the Taiga Shield ecozone.

CANADA'S ECOZONES

Canada has five major ecozone categories. Like the shields, however, these categories can be broken down into specific ecozones. The inset map shows where these ecozones are located.

Look closely at the map of the shield ecozones. Besides rock, what other features do these ecozones appear to have?

- Pacific Maritime
- Montane Cordillera
- Boreal Cordillera
- Taiga Cordillera
- Taiga Plains
- Boreal Plains
- Hudson Plains
- Prairie
- Taiga Shield
- Boreal Shield
- Mixedwood Plains
- Atlantic Maritime
- Southern Arctic
- Northern Arctic
- Arctic Cordillera

Nunavut

Yellowknife

Northwest Territories

Lake Athabasca   Uranium City

Selwyn Lake

Southern Indian Lake

Reindeer Lake

Churchill River

Nelson River

Manitoba

Flin Flon

Island Lake

Big Trout Lake

Lake Winnipeg   Sandy Lake

Saskatchewan

Lac Seul

Lake of the Woods

UNITED STATES

Thunder Bay

N

| 0 | 1,000 | 2,000 | kilometres |
| 0 | 500 | 1,000 | miles |

N

UNITED STATES

Hudson
Bay

Ungava
Bay

Newfoundland
and Labrador

Quebec

Smallwood
Reservoir

Churchill Falls

Labrador City

James
Bay

Manicouagan
Reservoir

St. John's

Manicouagan
River

Long Range
Mountains

Saguenay
River

Ontario

Avalon
Peninsula

Chicoutimi

Laurentian
Highlands

Lake
Nipigon

Lake Atibiti

Rouyn-Noranda

Lake
Superior

Sault Ste. Marie

Ottawa River

St. Lawrence
River

Atlantic
Ocean

Sudbury

Lake
Huron

Georgian Bay

Lake
Michigan

Shield Features

Shields are named for the rock mass that forms their base, so both the Taiga and Boreal Shield ecozones share this feature. These two ecozones also have other features in common. However, each has its own distinctions due to its location in Canada.

Forests

The words "taiga" and "boreal" both refer to forest growth, and forests are a main feature of both ecozones. The forests of these ecozones contain mainly coniferous trees. These trees have cones and needles instead of leaves, and remain green year round. Most of the trees in the Boreal Shield grow to full height. Many trees in the Taiga Shield are stunted in growth due to the colder climate.

Boreal forests cover much of Newfoundland's Terra Nova National Park.

A wetland works like a sponge in the way it gathers water. It releases its stores of water during dry seasons.

Wetlands

Wetlands are places where the soil is drenched with water at least part of the year. Wetlands water can come from nearby lakes, rivers, streams, or oceans. It can also come from rainfall, snowmelt, or **groundwater**. Four types of wetlands can be found in the shield ecozones. Bogs are areas of soggy ground filled with moss or plant matter called peat. Fens are peat-filled areas that support a variety of plant life, such as grasses and wildflowers. Marshes are wetlands that do not contain peat. They are home to many types of grasses. Swamps are similar to marshes, but they contain trees and shrubs instead of grasses.

Lakes in the Boreal Shield range in size from large to small. Some lakes are so small that they have not even been given names.

Eskers

An esker is a long ridge of gravel and sand. Like the lakes of the shield ecozones, eskers developed as a result of glacier deposits. Sand and gravel were deposited by streams and rivers that flowed on top of the glacier or, in some cases, in tunnels beneath the ice. The Taiga Shield ecozone has the highest concentration of eskers in Canada. Eskers are found in the Boreal Shield ecozone as well.

Most eskers are only a few kilometres long. Some, however, can extend hundreds of kilometres.

Freshwater Lakes

The Taiga and Boreal Shield ecozones are home to thousands of freshwater lakes. These lakes are a result of the massive glacier coverage the area once had. When the glaciers began receding, they left big craters in the ground. Water from melting glaciers as well as precipitation gathered into these depressions, forming the lakes that exist today.

FASCINATING FACTS

The word *boreal* comes from the Greek god Boreas. He is the god of the north wind that blows through these types of forests.

Taiga is a Russian word that means "marshy pine forest."

Peat is the main ingredient in garden soil mixes. Peat is useful in gardening because it has the ability to retain water yet still allow oxygen to reach plants.

Shield Climate

The shield ecozones cover a large expanse of land, from north to south and east to west. As a result, there is a wide range in climate within each ecozone as well as between the two.

Taiga Shield

The Taiga Shield ecozone has a subarctic climate, with cool summers and cold winters. Summer temperatures range from 7.5 degrees to 17.5 degrees Celsius. The growing season is only 120 days long. This ecozone is known for its summer sunshine, with up to 15 hours of daylight. Winter temperatures range from –25 degrees to –11 degrees Celsius. The cold climate creates survival challenges for many organisms over the long winter months. The days are dark in the wintertime, with only 8.5 hours of daylight. Being landlocked, the western part of the ecozone is much drier than the eastern part, which is near the Atlantic Ocean. Annual precipitation in the ecozone ranges from 200 millimetres in the west to 1,000 millimetres in Labrador. Snow covers the ground for six to eight months of the year.

Boreal Shield

Winter temperatures in the Boreal Shield ecozone depend on location and proximity to water. The presence of the Atlantic Ocean helps the eastern part of the ecozone have mild winters. Here, average temperatures are about –1 degree Celsius. The southern part of the ecozone, around the Great Lakes, also tends to have more **temperate** winters. The western part of the ecozone, however, has colder winter temperatures, with an average temperature of –20 degrees Celsius. Summer temperatures in the ecozone average about 13 degrees Celsius. The Boreal Shield receives more precipitation than the Taiga Shield, but is also influenced by location. The west receives about 400 millimetres each year, while the east, with the help of the Atlantic Ocean, can receive as much as 1,600 millimetres annually. These increased levels are called ocean effect precipitation.

Winter can bring much snow to the boreal forests of northern Saskatchewan.

Ocean Effect Precipitation

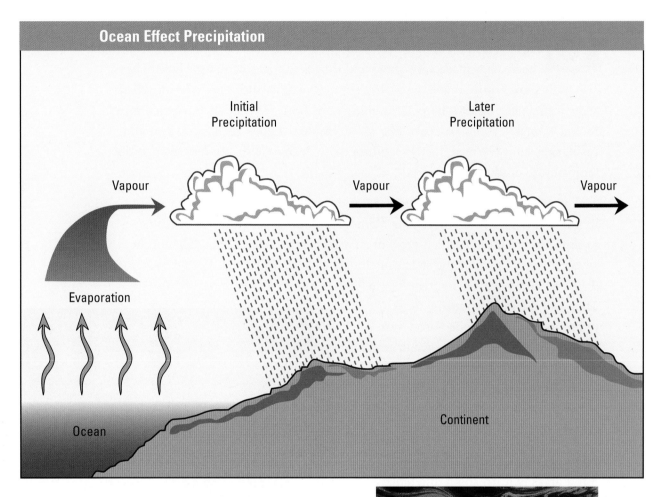

Initial Precipitation

Later Precipitation

Vapour

Vapour

Vapour

Evaporation

Ocean

Continent

The air over large bodies of water contains more moisture than the air over land. This moisture, or water vapour, forms clouds and may fall as precipitation over land. This precipitation can take the form of rain or snow.

FASCINATING FACTS

Permafrost is found throughout the Taiga Shield ecozone. Few plants can grow in this permanently frozen ground.

The climate of the Boreal Shield is also heavily influenced by Hudson Bay. Cold air masses from the bay bring high levels of precipitation to the area.

Shield Technology

One hundred years ago, few people ventured into the vast boreal forest. However, the Woodland Cree **adapted** to the hard living conditions found there. They made snowshoes and sleighs to travel across the land. They also built snow houses called *quin-zhee*. To make a quin-zhee, the Cree shovelled snow into a pile and let it harden for at least one hour. Then, they burrowed into the snow, making a hollow, cave-like space. Inside the quin-zhee, body heat and **insulating** snow warmed the temperature to –1 degree Celsius—warmer than the temperature outdoors.

Today, new technologies help scientists study the boreal forest and learn about its plants, animals, and **ecosystems**. Remote satellite sensing uses satellite images to show the types of trees that grow in an area, where wetlands and lakes occur, where fires are burning, the effects of climate change, and areas affected by human development. Scientists use remote satellite sensing to maintain healthy forests.

They also use remote sensing to monitor, map, and model forest fires. **Infrared** satellite images show burning vegetation. They show the location of active forest fires, how the fire is behaving or moving, and the size of the area that has been burned.

Scientists often study samples from forest areas to learn about different organisms and how many species live there. They use live traps and nets to collect birds and animals. Scientists record the age, gender, condition, and weight of each animal. They also mark animals with identification tags or bands. Scientists use the data they collect to understand how ecosystems change over time.

Forest fires are one of the greatest dangers the boreal forests face.

Satellite images provide scientists with much information about an area.

Scientists also use radio telemetry, radio tagging, or radio tracking. A transmitter attached to an animal sends a signal to a receiver. Scientists use the radio signal to track the animal's movements. This method of tracking provides information about an animal's habitat, territory, **migration**, activity, and life history.

FASCINATING FACTS

If the sky is cloudy, forest fires might not be detected with remote sensing monitors.

Scientists often use a Global Positioning System (GPS) to navigate the boreal forest. GPS uses satellite technology to find exact locations any place on Earth.

LIFE IN THE SHIELD

The shield ecozones are home to many species of plants and animals. These life forms have successfully adapted to harsh conditions in their environment, including permafrost, cool summers, and short growing seasons.

REPTILES

Reptiles are cold-blooded animals. This means they rely on their surroundings to regulate their temperature. Snakes and turtles are examples of reptiles. No reptiles live in the Taiga Shield due to its cold climate. The Boreal Shield, however, is home to both turtles and snakes, including the painted turtle and the maritime garter snake.

The painted turtle is named for the yellow and red markings that run across its body and shell.

PLANTS

Plants need water, sunlight, and **nutrients** from the soil to grow. The shield ecozones generally have a short growing season. Low temperatures, low precipitation, and high winds encourage low-growing and dwarf plants and trees in the Taiga Shield. The Boreal Shield is known for its forests of birch, aspen, spruce, pine and fir. Shrubs are plentiful in these ecozones, too.

The leaves on a trembling aspen move with the slightest breeze. When this occurs, the trees appear to tremble. This is how the tree received its name.

Snails prefer a moist environment. A snail will hide in its shell when the weather is dry and wait for moist weather to arrive.

INVERTEBRATES

Invertebrates are animals without an internal skeleton. Without a backbone or spine to give them structural support, some invertebrates carry an external skeleton called an **exoskeleton**. Snails and clams are invertebrates that use external shells for support and protection. Both of these animals are found in the shield ecozones. Insects are invertebrates that carry an exoskeleton made of **chitin**. Many invertebrates, including worms, do not have a skeleton at all.

The Atlantic puffin can have problems getting into the air and landing on the ground. It has been known to have crash landings.

AMPHIBIANS

Amphibians live in moist environments, and most spend a large amount of time in water. A few species of frogs are found in the Taiga Shield ecozone, including the mink and wood frogs. Due to its warmer climate, the Boreal Shield ecozone is home to several amphibian species, including the northern leopard frog, yellow-spotted salamander, and eastern newt.

The yellow-spotted salamander can be up to 20 centimetres in length.

BIRDS

The Taiga and Boreal shield ecozones are home to a variety of birds, from birds of prey, forest birds, and waterfowl to songbirds, shorebirds, and seabirds. In addition to their regular residents, the shield ecozones have many migrating birds passing through. Some birds stop to breed and raise their young in the area before migrating south for the winter.

Shield Plants

Sedges

Sedges are plants that resemble grasses. They differ from grasses by their triangular, solid stems and leaves that are arranged in groups of three instead of two. Their flowers consist of spikes found in the plant's upper sections. Sedges grow in clumps and are useful for erosion control. Small mammals, such as hares, graze on sedges, while small birds and waterfowl eat their seeds. One of the most common sedges found in the shield ecozones is cottongrass.

Blueberries grow in clusters and range in size from a small pea to a marble.

Shrubs

Shrubs are common in both the Taiga and Boreal Shield ecozones, and are widely used by many animals. Some varieties produce tasty berries, such as blueberries and cranberries, that animals eat. Shrubs also provide cover for wildlife, protecting animals from wind, weather, and predators.

Mosses

Mosses are small, low-growing, soft plants that commonly grow in clumps or mats. Mosses grow in damp or shady locations and are found throughout the shield ecozones. Sphagnum moss is one of the most common mosses found here.

Cottongrass grows mostly in peat bogs.

Black spruce can often be found growing in poorly drained areas, such as bogs and swamps.

Trees

Black spruce has shallow roots that do not reach deep permafrost layers. It is found in both of the shield ecozones. This tree is well suited for bogs and other poorly drained soils. The black spruce grows to about 18 metres high and is an important pulp and lumber tree in Canada. The towering paper birch grows in both ecozones as well. This tree gets its name from its white bark, which eventually peels off in papery sheets. The paper birch can grow to be 24 metres tall and can live up to 140 years. The jack pine's crown is gnarled when grown in harsh conditions, which is often the case in shield ecozones. The jack pine does not usually grow straight. This gives it a rugged look.

FASCINATING FACTS

Animals feed on the branches, leaves, and berries of many varieties of shrubs all year long. Nipping off the tips of a shrub's branches encourages the plant to bush out.

Canada's Aboriginal Peoples put the resin from black spruce on wounds to help them heal quickly.

Sphagnum moss can hold up to 20 times its weight in water.

Birds and Mammals

Waterfowl

The many wetlands of the shield ecozones attract waterfowl, such as ducks, loons, swans, and geese. These birds have webbed feet close to the rear of their bodies to help them swim. They also have flattened bills to grab the plants they eat. Ducks have different feeding styles. Dabbling ducks, including the American black duck, stay on the surface, dip their bills, and shake their heads. Diving ducks, such as the ring-necked duck, head to deeper waters. They dive deep down into the water to catch fish. Then, they return to the surface.

The ring-necked duck can dive 12 metres into the water to catch fish.

Northern flickers will search for food in tree trunks as well as on the ground.

Ground-dwelling Birds

The forests of the shield ecozones attract ground-dwelling birds, such as ptarmigans, as well as those that live in trees, such as woodpeckers. Ptarmigans change colour with the seasons in order to camouflage themselves from predators. In summer, ptarmigans are brown with gold flecks. In fall, their colouring becomes grey. In winter, their feathers turn pure white. The northern flicker is a type of woodpecker. Unlike most woodpeckers that find their food in trees, the northern flicker often forages on the ground for its food.

Weasels often move into the dens of animals they have successfully hunted.

Mammals

Many mammals are found in the shield ecozones. Large land dwellers range from **herbivores**, such as moose, caribou, and deer, to large **carnivores**, including polar, grizzly, and black bears as well as lynxes and wolves. Smaller plant-eating animals include beavers, hares, marmots, raccoons, chipmunks, skunks, and voles. Foxes, weasels, river otters, coyotes, martens, wolverines, and muskrats are the smaller carnivores of the shield ecozones.

Shorebirds and Seabirds

Shorebirds and seabirds, such as sandpipers, terns, gulls, puffins, and killdeer, are found where the land meets the ocean and Hudson Bay. Shorebirds feed and nest along the banks and shores of the ocean waters. Seabirds frequent coastal waters and the open ocean, far from shore.

FASCINATING FACTS

Hundreds of thousands of caribou migrate through the Taiga Shield each year. They sometimes follow long, winding eskers on their migration route.

Songbirds of the shield ecozones include jays, magpies, crows, tree swallows, sparrows, ravens, warblers, and doves. Osprey, owls, hawks, and eagles are the region's birds of prey.

Polar bears roam the coastal regions of the Taiga Shield ecozone in summer. They move to pack ice in winter.

Fish, Invertebrates, Amphibians, and Reptiles

Invertebrates

Invertebrates, creatures without a backbone, are some of the smallest creatures of the shield ecozones. The region is home to an abundance of insects, especially during the summer breeding months in wetland areas. Billions of flying, biting insects, from mosquitoes and black flies to no-see-ums live in these ecozones. Other invertebrates of the shield ecozones include snails, clams, and a few species of butterfly.

Pike can grow up to 1.5 metres in length.

Fish

There are three types of fish swimming in the fresh waters of the shield ecozones. Predatory fish, such as pike, sturgeon, bass, walleye, and trout, eat other fish. The fish they eat are called prey fish. These fish include lake herring, lake whitefish, rainbow smelt, and yellow perch. Sometimes, ocean-dwelling fish enter the fresh water bodies to **spawn**. These fish are called **anadramous** fish. They include several varieties of lamprey as well as Atlantic salmon.

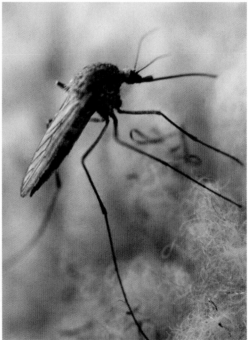

The word *mosquito* means "little fly" in Spanish.

Reptiles and Amphibians

The Taiga Shield ecozone is too harsh for reptiles to survive, but the Boreal Shield is home to two varieties of garter snake, as well as the red belly snake. Several species of turtle can also be found here. Amphibians can be found in both ecozones. They even have some species in common. The mink frog and blue-spotted salamander live in both the Taiga and Boreal Shield ecozones. Mink frogs are named for the odour they emit, which is similar to that of a mink. The smell is much like rotting onions.

Mink frogs spend the cold winter months underwater, at the bottom of their home pond or lake.

FASCINATING FACTS

A distinguishing feature of all reptiles is their armour of scales. Scales are made of keratin, like human fingernails, and are generally directed backwards. Differing in size and shape, scales can be used to identify types of reptiles.

Salamanders are amphibians, but they look like lizards, a type of reptile. The main difference between the two is that salamanders do not have scales.

"No-see-ums" is the name given to tiny, black biting insects that fly. Their real name is "biting midges." Probably the smallest biting fly in Canada, no-see-ums can send herds of caribou running to avoid their vicious sting.

Northern pike are large predatory fish. They are sometimes called "freshwater sharks." Northern pike are known as aggressive fighters.

Shield Ecozones in Danger

The shield ecozones have been affected by human development. Some of the changes this development has brought to the region are threatening the plants and animals that live there, and the environment itself. The largest impact in recent years has been made by logging and the forestry industry.

Logging is the dominant industrial activity in Canada's forests and plays a key role in the country's economy.

The James Bay Hydroelectric Project was started in 1971. Even though it has not finished construction, it is still one of the largest hydro-electric projects in the world.

There is little land in the shield ecozones that has not been altered by human settlement or industries. More than 50 percent of the land in the central Canadian Shield has been logged, and more trees will be cut down in the future. Clear-cutting is a logging technique in which all of the trees in an area are removed at once. It destroys habitat and disrupts normal forest growth. Plant and animal species lose their natural habitats as the boreal forests gradually disappear. In most cases, trees are being cut down faster than new trees have a chance to grow. Many forests are left with only aspen and birch trees instead of the coniferous trees that originally covered the land.

Another threat to the animals in the region is the construction of hydro-electric dams. Normally built on major rivers, the dams change the water flow. The change floods thousands of hectares of land. This destroys habitats and migration routes for many animals, including caribou. Large numbers of wildlife drown or become displaced. The James Bay Hydroelectric Project, in Quebec, has caused the drowning deaths of thousands of migrating caribou.

FASCINATING FACTS

The forestry industry occurs mostly in the boreal forests of Quebec and Ontario.

Due to the forestry industry, the world's boreal forests are experiencing deforestation as rapidly as rain forests.

WORKING IN THE SHIELD

With their forests, wetlands, and fresh waters, the shield ecozones present opportunities in several career areas. The forestry industry is a major employer in these areas. The areas also attract scientists from various fields who spend their time studying the ecosystems that make up these ecozones.

FORESTER

- Duties: works to ensure people use forests wisely and limit harm to forest habitat and wildlife

- Education: bachelor's, master's, or doctoral degree in forestry

- Interests: forest ecosystems, land use, habitat restoration, wildlife conservation, botany

Foresters work for government agencies and forestry companies as researchers and consultants. They plan forest use, forest-renewal projects, and advise about appropriate forest-management techniques. They assess the effects of pollution, human activities, and forest fires on forest habitats and wildlife.

WETLAND ECOLOGIST

- Duties: studies wetland ecology and works to protect wetlands

- Education: bachelor's or master's degree in ecological science

- Interests: animals, plants, working outdoors, and science

Wetland ecologists spend time in muddy wetlands. They take water samples, count birds, or gather data. Wetland ecologists analyze this information to determine the health of the wetlands. They also learn how the area has changed over time. Wetland ecologists help plan and implement programs that restore wetlands to their natural state.

PALEOLIMNOLOGIST

- Duties: studies past freshwater life and environments

- Education: master's or doctorate degree in geology, ecology, or biology

- Interests: history of aquatic plant and animal life, conservation, environment, biology, and geology

Paleolimnologists drill into lake **sediment** and pull out cylinders, or cores, of this sediment. They study the mud cores to learn about the past life in this freshwater environment. Paleolimnologists study the effects of pollution and acid rain on freshwater ecosystems. Their findings help environmental consultants and freshwater biologists.

ECO CHALLENGE

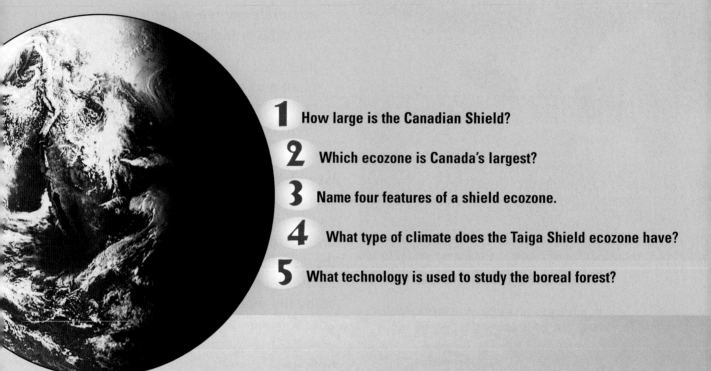

1 How large is the Canadian Shield?

2 Which ecozone is Canada's largest?

3 Name four features of a shield ecozone.

4 What type of climate does the Taiga Shield ecozone have?

5 What technology is used to study the boreal forest?

6 What is a an invertebrate?

7 What is a sedge?

8 Name the three types of bear that are found in the shield ecozones.

9 What type of reptiles are found in the Taiga Shield ecozone?

10 What is clear-cutting?

Answers

1. Approximately 4.8 million square kilometres, or about half the size of Canada
2. The Boreal Shield ecozone
3. Forests, wetlands, freshwater lakes, eskers
4. A subarctic climate
5. Remote satellite sensing and infrared imaging
6. An animal without an internal skeleton
7. A plant that resembles grass
8. Grizzly, black, and polar bears
9. None. The environment is too harsh for reptiles to survive.
10. A logging technique in which all of the trees in an area are removed at once

TESTING THE SOIL

Soil in the shield ecozones is acidic. This limits the types of plants that can thrive and survive there. The composition of soil affects its ability to hold moisture and provide the nutrients needed for plants to grow. This experiment will help you learn what types of soil are best for plant growing.

MATERIALS

- 3 soil samples (include a variety of samples, such as garden soil, clay, and sand)
- trowel
- 3 small flower pots with saucers
- water
- bean seeds
- tall stakes
- pen or pencil
- ruler
- paper
- tape

1. Gather samples of different soils, and fill a flowerpot with each kind. Label your flowerpots to describe the soil inside.

2. Water the soil, and then plant two or three bean seeds in each. Put a stake in each pot for the beans to climb. Keep the pots moist while the beans sprout.

3. Notice which beans sprout first. Measure the height of the plants every few days until the beans flower. Record this information on a chart. Use this data to determine which soil had the best growing conditions.

FURTHER RESEARCH

How can I find out more about the Canadian Shield and the shield ecozones?

- Libraries have books about the geography, plants, and animals of Canada.

- Nature and science centres are places to learn more about Canada's ecozones.

- The Internet offers websites on Canadian geography, and plant and animal life, including videos and maps.

BOOKS

Watson, Galadriel. *Wetlands*. New York, NY: Weigl Publishers Inc., 2006.

Miller-Schroeder, Patrician. *Boreal Forests*. New York, NY: Weigl Publishers Inc., 2006.

Schwartzenberger, Tina. *The Canadian Shield* (Canadian Geographic Regions). Calgary, AB: Weigl Educational Publishers Limited, 2006.

WEBSITES

Where can I learn more about the Canadian Shield?

How Stuff Works
http://videos.howstuffworks.com/hsw/5471-canada-the-canadian-shield-video.htm

Where can I learn more about the shield's ecozones?

The Canadian Biodiversity Website
www.canadianbiodiversity.mcgill.ca

Where can I find out more about protecting boreal forest areas?

The Taiga Rescue Network
www.taigarescue.org

Airdrie Public Library

GLOSSARY

adapted: changed over time to suit the environment

anadramous: fish that breed in fresh water but live their lives in the sea

carnivores: animals whose main diet consists of meat

chitin: a hard material made out of carbohydrates, which forms the exoskeleton of various organisms such as insects, arthropods, and crustaceans

ecosystems: communities of living things sharing an environment

erosion: the process of wearing away

exoskeleton: an external skeleton

groundwater: underground water that has come from the seepage of surface water

herbivores: animals whose diet consists mainly of plants

infrared: invisible wavelengths

insulating: keeping heat in or out

migration: moving with the seasons from one area to another

nutrients: substances that provide nourishment

organisms: living things

Precambrian: a period that occurred 4,500 to 543 million years ago

sediment: the matter that settles to the bottom of a liquid

spawn: to lay eggs

temperate: a moderate climate, neither hot nor cold

tree line: the upper limit of where trees can grow

tundra: a vast, mostly flat, treeless, arctic region in which the subsoil is permanently frozen

INDEX